BEAVERS

Published by Smart Apple Media

1980 Lookout Drive, North Mankato, Minnesota 56003

Design and Production by The Design Lab/Kathy Petelinsek

Photographs by Premiere Stock & Fine Art, Tom Stack & Associates, Visuals Unlimited

Library of Congress Cataloging-in-Publication Data

Frisch, Aaron.

Beavers / by Aaron Frisch

p. cm. -- (Northern Trek)

Includes resources, glossary, and index

Summary: Describes the physical characteristics, behavior, and habitat of the North American beaver.

ISBN 1-58340-030-3

1. American beaver–Juvenile literature. [1. American beaver. 2. Beavers.] I. Title.

II. Series: Northern Trek (Mankato, Minn.)

QL737.R632 F75   2000

599.37–dc21   99-049589

First Edition

2 4 6 8 9 7 5 3 1

NORTHERN TREK

BEAVERS

WRITTEN BY AARON FRISCH

SMART APPLE MEDIA

Few animals work quite as hard as the beaver. It is a diver, a lumberjack, and a carpenter. The durable stick dams that it builds across streams and rivers have amazed humans for centuries. It also has played a major role in American history, providing clothes for early explorers and Native Americans and serving as a central means of trade. Beavers never seem to rest from cutting down trees, collecting branches for food, or building dams, thus the expression, "busy as a beaver." Today, millions of these hardworking mammals are spread across North America.

THE BEAVER (*Castor candensis*) belongs to the rodent family, though it is much bigger than most of its relatives. Full-grown males and females are about the same size, making it difficult to tell them apart. Adult beavers are about two and a half feet (76 cm) long, not including a 12-inch (30 cm) tail. They usually weigh about 55 pounds (25 kg), though they can tip the scales at more than 70 pounds (32 kg).

Beavers live by ponds and slow-moving rivers and streams near woodlands. They spend most of their time in the water. Although they look rather clumsy when walking, beavers are fantastic swimmers. Their webbed back paws and strong hind legs propel them easily through the water. The flat, scaly tail is used mainly as a **rudder**, but it can also be used as a paddle for bursts of speed. The beaver's front paws are small and delicate, almost like hands. With these paws, the beaver can carry small sticks or pack

A paddle-like tail and large, compact body make the beaver the most identifiable member of the rodent family.

mud when building a dam. A beaver can stay underwater for as long as 15 minutes before coming to the surface for air.

Near the beaver's hind end are a pair of **glands** that produce a strong-smelling oil. The beaver uses this oil to grease its reddish-brown coat, making the fur waterproof. The beaver's big body and thick, oiled coat keep it warm as it swims in and out of icy water, even during the coldest winters.

One of the beaver's most recognizable features is its pair of large front teeth. These teeth, which are covered by a hard, orange-brown **enamel**, never stop growing. When a beaver chews on a tree, they are sharpened and worn down at the

With their waterproof fur and great swimming skills, beavers are one of the few mammals that are more at home in water than on land.

If a beaver does not keep its teeth worn down to the proper length, the teeth will grow so long that the beaver will be unable to eat and will starve to death. To prevent this, beavers must continually gnaw on wood.

same time. With chisel-shaped teeth and powerful jaw muscles, an adult beaver can cut down a tree more than 16 inches (40 cm) thick within hours.

It is usually nighttime when beavers cut down the trees they need for food and building materials. To fell a tree, a beaver stands on its hind legs, using its tail for balance. It works its way around the tree, biting chunks out of it from all sides to create an hourglass-shaped cut. Beavers normally cut down trees that are close to the water.

Beavers are strong enough to cut and haul almost any kind– and size–of tree found near North American wetlands.

Few animal-made structures are as impressive or durable as the dams built by beavers. Dams may be more than 100 yards (91 m) long and may dramatically change the water level and appearance of major rivers.

Once the tree falls, they chew the branches off and push or pull the pieces into the water.

Beavers eat only vegetables and bark. In the spring and summer, many types of soft plants are available to eat, including water lilies, grasses, and leaves. As the green plants of summer start to die, beavers begin collecting freshly cut tree branches and form them into piles at the bottom of the pond or stream. When the water freezes over in the winter, the beavers swim to this stock of food beneath the ice and feed on the bark. Most animals cannot **digest** tree bark, but beavers have unique **microorganisms** in their stomachs that help them to break the bark down.

Beavers have outstanding building skills. To make their homes, called lodges, beavers look for a high river bank. If they find one, they then dig one or more tunnels that open up into a wide chamber in the soil. More often, though, the beavers build the lodge themselves, creating a large mound of branches and mud with a dry den inside. Finished lodges are so strongly built that even the largest **predators** can't break into them.

Because lodge entrances are always underwater, beavers need deep water. If a river or stream is too shallow, they may build a dam to raise the water level. To start a dam, beavers push long, thick sticks into the river bottom. Then they build a wall

The fur of beaver kits looks fluffier than the fur of adults. That is because beavers cannot produce oil to grease their coats until they are a few months old.

of branches, stones, and mud around this foundation. If part of a dam breaks or a lodge is damaged, beavers will immediately work on it until it is fixed. Although beaver dams can sometimes cause problems for humans by flooding roads or farmers' crops, they also benefit many other animals—including otters, moose, ducks, and turtles—by developing essential pond **habitats**.

Beavers live in family groups of five to ten individuals. Mating takes place underwater in the winter, and a litter of up to eight babies—called kits—are born late in the spring. The kits stay inside the lodge for their first six weeks and do not begin to eat twigs or bark until they are a

Beavers spend most of their lives working on dams and lodges. To get the energy they need, the furry builders must eat huge amounts of food.

Beaver pelts were extremely valuable to the first American settlers. In the early 1700s, a trapper could trade 12 beaver pelts for a new rifle, a very expensive item in those days. Today, few beavers are trapped.

month old. Most kits are afraid of the water, and mother beavers often have to carry them into the water to make them learn to swim.

Despite their large size and powerful bite, beavers need to be on the lookout for wolves, coyotes, bears, and other large predators. Because they are slow runners and have poor eyesight, beavers stay as close to the safety of the water as possible when cutting down trees. If a beaver senses danger, it warns other members of its family by smacking its tail on the surface of the water. This signal can be heard up to a half-mile (.8 km) away.

As many as 200 million beavers were once spread from the Arctic Circle all the way to northern Mexico. Native Americans relied on them for their fur in making clothing. When Europeans began to

settle in America, the beaver trade began. Explorers trapped millions of the animals, whose valuable **pelts** were made into fine coats and **felt** hats. Many pelts were sent to Europe. Such a large number of beavers were trapped that the species was wiped out entirely in many parts of North America.

In the early 1900s, the United States government finally began giving beavers protection from hunters and trappers. Since that time, the beaver population has bounced back to healthy levels again throughout much of Canada and the United States. The stable number of beavers today ensures that these shy, hardworking rodents will continue to leave their mark on wetlands for many years to come.

While beaver pelts were once highly valued, few beavers are killed by hunters and trappers now. Because of this, and because few large predators are left in the wild, beavers can be found in nearly all North American wetlands.

BEAVERS ARE FASCINATING

to view. Once they get used to human visitors, they tend to allow spectators to watch them as they go about their work, building dams and lodges. Because of overtrapping in the 19th century, beavers disappeared from much of their range. Thanks to conservation efforts, however, they've made a comeback and are now found throughout the United States and Canada. Listed here are some beaver habitats with public access. As with any trek into nature, it is important to remember that wild animals are unpredictable and can be dangerous if approached. The best way to view wildlife is from a respectful—and safe—distance.

PARADISE POINT NATURE CENTER, HEBRON MARSH SANCTUARY IN NEW HAMPSHIRE *Visitors can follow a short wooded trail to watch beavers at work in a protected habitat.*

WOLF RIDGE ENVIRONMENTAL LEARNING CENTER IN FINLAND, MINNESOTA *Wolf Ridge is 1,400 acres of natural beauty located on a forested ridge that overlooks Lake Superior. Learning programs and summer camps take visitors into the heart of a vast wildlife community, which includes numerous streams and rivers that are home to beavers and other northern mammals.*

THE APPALACHIAN MOUNTAINS *This mountain range extends 1,600 miles (2,579 km) from Quebec in Canada all the way south to Alabama. The Appalachian National Scenic Trail, the longest continuous hiking trail in the world, passes through some excellent beaver habitats.*

THE GREAT LAKES REGION *Beavers are common throughout this area of lakes and forests. Michigan's Isle Royale National Park and Wisconsin's Nicollet National Forest offer some of the region's best opportunities to see beavers.*

digest: *the body's action of breaking down food for use*

enamel: *a hard substance that forms a thin layer over teeth*

felt: *a soft cloth made by combining wool and fur*

glands: *organs that produce bodily oils or fluids*

habitats: *places where plants or animals normally live*

microorganisms: *tiny creatures, some which live inside other animals*

pelts: *the skinned furs of animals*

predators: *animals that kill other animals for food*

rudder: *a flat object used to help steer a boat or swimmer*